For Heather and Adam

© Louise Cross 2019

Published 2019 by CWR, Waverley Abbey House, Waverley Lane, Farnham, Surrey GU9 8EP, UK. CWR is a Registered Charity – Number 294387 and a Limited Company registered in England – Registration Number 1990308.

The right of Louise Cross to be identified as the author and illustrator of this work has been asserted by her in accordance with the Copyright, Designs and Patents Act 1988.

For a list of National Distributors, visit cwr.org.uk/distributors

Scripture reference taken from The Holy Bible, International Children's Bible®, copyright © 1986, 1988, 1999, 2015 by Tommy Nelson™, a division of Thomas Nelson. Used with permission.

Concept development, editing, design and production by CWR.

Cover image: Louise Cross

Printed in the UK by Linney

ISBN: 978-1-78259-963-0

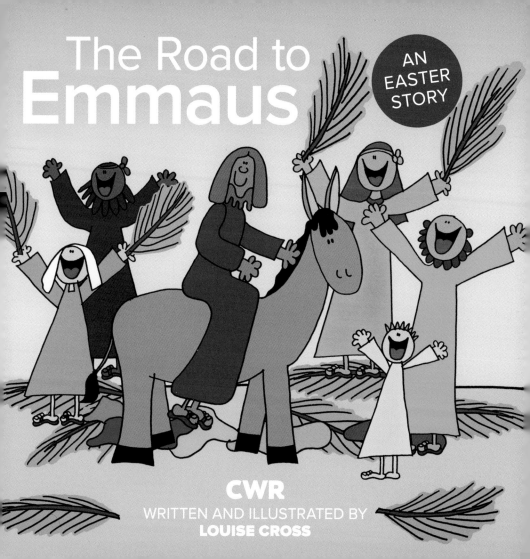

The Road to
Emmaus

AN EASTER STORY

CWR

WRITTEN AND ILLUSTRATED BY
LOUISE CROSS

Many years ago, two friends of Jesus were walking along the road to a town called Emmaus.

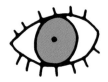

They walked along slowly, feeling very
sad, because they had just seen
some very sad things.
'Hey, let's not be sad,' said Cleopas to
his friend. 'I will try to cheer us up.
Could we play I-Spy?'
'No thanks, we've just played that one.'

'How about trying to spot the biggest donkey?'

'No, that's boring!'

'Tell you what, that's just reminded me. You loved that day when Jesus came to town riding on a donkey, didn't you?'

'Ooh, yes, I did – that was amazing.
All the people laid out their coats on the
floor like a carpet for Him to walk on.'
'Yes – and they laid out palm branches
as well. It was like He was the emperor
or something.
That was such a great day!'
'Yes, except He rode on a donkey,
not a chariot!'

The two friends kept on walking, remembering some happy times with Jesus.

'Do you remember all those miracles Jesus did too?'

'Yes. Yes, my favourite one was when that little boy brought his lunch with only five loaves and two fish, and Jesus fed five thousand men with it!

That was a yummy day...' said Cleopas, rubbing his tummy.

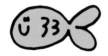

'But then, do you remember when the leaders of the town and the priests didn't like Jesus?'
'Yes, they all hated the things He did.'
'I know, but Jesus was always kind, wasn't He?'

'Yes, He really was – but even though He'd done those miracles and been kind and told us those amazing stories, all the people shouted, "Kill him!", didn't they?'

'Lots of people in the town wanted Jesus to die. That was so sad, wasn't it?'

Cleopas kicked a stone along the road. They were both feeling sad remembering what had happened just that Friday.

'Then they made Jesus wear a thorny crown on His head, didn't they, and they made Him carry that big wooden cross all the way through town and up to the top of the hill. There were crowds of people watching.'

'At the top of the hill, the soldiers nailed Jesus to the cross. They were so cruel. They put Him between two criminals.'
'Yes – one on the left, and one on the right.'

Cleopas got out his hanky to blow his nose and wipe his eyes because he was so sad.

'It was very, very sad. And then, remember, Jesus said, "Forgive them, Father, for they don't know what they are doing..."'

'After that, the whole town went dark,
right in the middle of the afternoon.'
'Yes, although I had my eyes shut for a
long time because I couldn't look
at Jesus.
What happened next?'

'Well, when Jesus had died, they lowered His body down and carefully wrapped it up in a big cloth. A man from Arimathea was really kind and offered to put Jesus' body in his special tomb.'

'A tomb – what's that?'

'It's a bit like a cave. He put Jesus' body inside, and then they rolled a big stone across the entrance so nobody could get in.'

'Oh yes, and then they put some soldiers outside it to guard it. They didn't want any funny business, did they?'

'No, that's right. Do you feel any better yet, Cleopas?'

'Not really.'

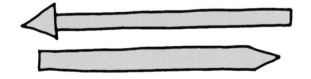

'Well, can you believe what our friend Mary and the other women said earlier? About the angels at the tomb, and how Jesus isn't there and He is alive? Can it be true, do you think?'

'I don't know... but wouldn't it be great if it was true?'

Suddenly, a man appeared on the road near them – but they were so sad they hardly even noticed him.

'Hello,' said the man, 'why are you so sad? What are you talking about?'

'Good grief!' said Cleopas, looking at the man. 'You must be the only one in Jerusalem who doesn't know all the things that have just happened!'

'On Friday, our best friend Jesus died. He died on a cross.'
'Yes, and they put His body in an empty tomb,' Cleopas butted in.
'Some of our friends said Jesus' body is missing. He's gone! We're so confused and upset – we don't know what to do. Why did Jesus even have to go through all that? It's just not fair!'

'Can't you two figure it out?' asked the man. 'Think about everything you have been told!'
He whipped out his handy pocket-sized book of Scriptures.

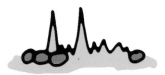

The man began to explain. 'Can't you remember what the prophets said back in the time before Jesus even came? Go way back to the days of Moses,' he said. 'Remember all those special messages God sent to the people. You need to believe all these things – they're all true!'

The man kept on talking and talking, and the three of them kept on walking and walking. The two friends both listened in amazement at everything the man was saying.

Soon they arrived at the town of Emmaus, and they were both feeling so much better.

As they got near to their house, the man they were talking with just kept on going. Cleopas called out, 'Goodness me, you can't go now – it's getting very late. Hey, why don't you come into our house for some supper?'

So the man went into their house with them, and they found some bread to eat. The man broke it in half in a special way and said, 'Thank You, God, for this food.'

Suddenly, the two friends recognised the man! It was JESUS – right there in front of them!
Their jaws dropped to the floor and their eyes nearly popped out of their heads!
But as soon as they recognised Him, Jesus disappeared – just like that!

The two friends were stunned. They even looked under the table for Jesus, but He had gone.

'Wowee! I can't believe it, Jesus is ALIVE – our other friends were right! Jesus is alive, and we've just chatted with Him. We've just had tea with Him!'

'But where's He gone?' asked Cleopas. 'I don't know, but we need to get back to Jerusalem and tell the others!'

'What, right now?' asked Cleopas.
'Yes, now – let's go. I feel so much better,' said his friend.
'I feel like there's fiery excitement in my tummy. Jesus is alive!'
'Jesus is alive. He has risen from the dead – it's a miracle!'
'I know, I'm so happy, happy, HAPPY. Come on, hurry up, let's go!'

So the two friends ran all the way back to Jerusalem. It was seven miles away and it was the middle of the night, but they didn't mind. They were just so excited!

When they arrived back in Jerusalem, they ran through the town and upstairs into the room where some other friends – the disciples – were gathered.

'Jesus is alive – we've seen Him!' they shouted.

'Are you sure?' asked one of the disciples.

'Yes, Jesus has risen from the dead. He showed Himself to us!' Cleopas insisted.

Then... POP! Right there and then,
Jesus appeared in the room
before their very eyes.
'Peace be with you,' He said.
The disciples thought He was a ghost!
'Aaahhhhh!' they cried. They were very
scared. Could it really be Jesus?

'Don't be frightened,' Jesus said gently.
'Look at my hands and my feet.
You can feel – I am real.'
The disciples stared and stared.
They couldn't believe it. They were all
looking at Him, and they could reach out
and touch Him. Their best friend was
alive again! Their best friend was here!
Now they really could believe it!

Then Jesus said, 'I am going back to heaven soon, and you will have a very important job to do. You have to tell everyone that I am ALIVE! I won't be here on earth anymore, but I will send you help and power from heaven, so you will be brave enough to tell everyone the good news.'

The disciples were so happy!
Goodness me, what a night they had.
Jesus was ALIVE, they had all seen
Him, and now they had hope and a
friend for ever.

Do you know that Jesus died on the cross and rose again because He loved every single one of us sooo much? Even though we can't see Jesus with our eyes, He can appear in our lives and give us an exciting fire in our tummies and be our special friend forever too! Why not read some more about the disciples' adventures in the book of Luke in the New Testament of the Bible.

Jesus said:

'Those who believe without seeing me will be truly happy.'

(John 20:29, International Children's Bible)